This journal belongs to:

_____

Dwell on the beauty of life.
Watch the stars, and see yourself running with them.

Marcus Aurelius

Dear Reader,

Thanks for purchasing our book.

We feel grateful to serve you with our carefully created:

The Writing Prompt Journal

& We hope you enjoy, learn and find what you're looking for.

All the best,

21 Exercises
& The True Potential Project Publishing Team

As a little thank you note,
*we've three **FREE** Personal-Growth exercises waiting for you.*

Simply send an email to to exercises21@yahoo.com
Title the email "Writing Prompt"

And we will send you Three Personal Development Hacks for FREE.

The Writing Prompt Journal

A creative Self-Discovery Guide

Follow us on Instagram
For promotions, giveaways and newest arrivals

Instagram: 21exercises_journals

Disclaimer
This book is not intended to be a substitute for medical advice or treatment. Any person with a condition requiring medical attention should consult a qualified medical practitioner or suitable therapist.
The information provided in this book is stated to be truthful and consistent, in that any liability, in terms of inattention or otherwise, by any usage or abuse of any policies, processes, or directions contained within is the solitary and utter responsibility of the recipient reader. Under no circumstances will any legal responsibility or blame be held against the publisher for any reparation, damages, or monetary loss due to the information herein, either directly or indirectly.

The Writing Prompt Journal

A Creative Self-Discovery Guide

Created by:

21 Exercises

A Message From The Authors

What better way than using creativity for a journey of self-discovery.
Forget, for now, another self-help book, another seminar or another
motivational YouTube video.

It starts and ends with you.

The answer has, is and always will be within.

Be creative to open the doors of infinite wisdom.

Introduction

Creativity
/ˌkriːeɪˈtɪvɪti/

noun

The ability to produce original and unusual ideas,
or to make something new or imaginative

This journal is not intended to set you upon a tough road of self-discovery. Don't get us wrong, working on yourself will inevitably lead to tough situations, uncomfortable conversations and painful realizations. But self-discovery is also a journey of joy, heightened awareness and (literally) discovering new territories.

To find inspiration and new insights we all have an amazing power within us: *creativity*. It is not equally developed in all of us, but we *all* have access to it. Naturally, creativity could be used to make art, solve difficult tasks at work or even something as 'simple' as organizing a dinner party. It is the ability to produce original and unusual ideas or to make something new or imaginative. And thus, it could also magnificently assist you on your journey of self-discovery.

Creativity needs space, time and a safe environment to flourish. It's absolutely not about being perfect or doing it exactly right. Not in the slightest way. Freedom of self-expression is all you need.

And *that* is exactly what makes it so difficult to be creative. We are so conditioned to be perfect, not making mistakes, *fit* within the conditions of society.Self-expression is harnessed and mocked most of the time. But who are we if we don't genuinely express ourselves?

This journal is an accessible way to practice creativity. The writing prompts all have a self-discovery nature. So you could practice and improve your creativity in an easy and fun way. You will definitely gain some new insights about all areas of your life, your place in this world and life in general. Above all enjoy the writing, enjoy being creative, enjoy discovering new territories and first and foremost enjoy expressing yourself. The benefits will be refreshing and empowering. It doesn't have to be perfect, it just has to be you.

How To Use This Journal

On every page, you'll find two writing prompts. This could be a question, a statement, an exercise or a quote. Contrary to the header of this page, there is no specific *how-to* for using this journal. Creativity can not be caged. It is up to you to make something out of these writing prompts. You don't need a specific guideline or permission to express yourself.

What we do recommend though, is to find a time and space where you can use this journal in all freedom. Do it with attention to experience the most joy and best results. If you want to do one writing prompt a day then we recommend to use a specific time each day. For example during your morning routine, at the beginning of the evening or before you go to bed. Pickin a specific time each day is the fastest way to integrate a daily habit.

There is enough space to finish each prompt. If you need more space to write than you could use the blank lined pages at the end of this journal.

Lastly, enjoy the use of this journal and let creativity bring you to new, undiscovered territory.

How tomorrow would look like if you had twenty percent more courage.

_____
_____
_____
_____
_____
_____
_____
_____
_____
_____
_____
_____
_____
_____

A dialogue between you and your criticizing Self.

_____
_____
_____
_____
_____
_____
_____
_____
_____
_____
_____
_____
_____
_____
_____
_____

"If you tell the truth, you don't have to remember anything."
Mark Twain

_____
_____
_____
_____
_____
_____
_____
_____
_____
_____
_____
_____
_____

The value of delaying gratification.

_____
_____
_____
_____
_____
_____
_____
_____
_____
_____
_____
_____
_____
_____
_____

The 3 things you actually should do this year.

_____
_____
_____
_____
_____
_____
_____
_____
_____
_____
_____
_____
_____
_____

The difference between gratitude and positive thinking.

_____
_____
_____
_____
_____
_____
_____
_____
_____
_____
_____
_____
_____
_____

A movie has been made of your life so far. Write a synopsis.

_____

_____

_____

_____

_____

_____

_____

_____

_____

_____

_____

_____

A roadmap for dealing with rejection.

Three of your most amazing strengths.

_____
_____
_____
_____
_____
_____
_____
_____
_____
_____
_____
_____
_____

A dialogue between you and your (future) partner.

_____
_____
_____
_____
_____
_____
_____
_____
_____
_____
_____
_____
_____
_____
_____

"The truth is rarely pure and never simple."
Oscar Wilde, *The Importance of Being Earnest*

_____
_____
_____
_____
_____
_____
_____
_____
_____
_____
_____
_____
_____

A weekly food diary of your most healthy self.

_____
_____
_____
_____
_____
_____
_____
_____
_____
_____
_____
_____
_____

Your next holiday.

_____
_____
_____
_____
_____
_____
_____
_____
_____
_____
_____
_____

A precious childhood memory.

_____
_____
_____
_____
_____
_____
_____
_____
_____
_____
_____
_____
_____

The difference between love and loyalty.

Your fears in a nutshell.

A day full of joy.

_____

How you could deal with all your worries at once.

_____

> "The unexamined life is not worth living."
> Socrates

_____
_____
_____
_____
_____
_____
_____
_____
_____
_____
_____
_____

A synopsis about the book that you need to write.

_____
_____
_____
_____
_____
_____
_____
_____
_____
_____
_____

A roadmap for dealing with failure.

.

A synopsis about the book that you need to write.

_____
_____
_____
_____
_____
_____
_____
_____
_____
_____
_____
_____
_____
_____

A poem about your first love experience.

_____
_____
_____
_____
_____
_____
_____
_____
_____
_____
_____
_____
_____
_____

A life-changing scene about the 16-year old you.

_____
_____
_____
_____
_____
_____
_____
_____
_____
_____
_____
_____
_____
_____
_____

> "Don't spend time beating on a wall,
> hoping to transform it into a door."
> coco chanel

Three past memories that make your life unique.

Advice about life, that will change everything.

_____

_____

_____

_____

_____

_____

_____

_____

_____

_____

_____

_____

_____

_____

The weekly spending habit of a millionaire.

A motivating morning routine.

_____
_____
_____
_____
_____
_____
_____
_____
_____
_____
_____
_____
_____
_____

Daily reflection routine at night.

_____
_____
_____
_____
_____
_____
_____
_____
_____
_____
_____
_____
_____
_____
_____
_____

What if you were three years younger?

_____
_____
_____
_____
_____
_____
_____
_____
_____
_____
_____
_____
_____

"So comes snow after fire, and even dragons have their endings."
J.R.R. Tolkien, The Hobbit

_____
_____
_____
_____
_____
_____
_____
_____
_____
_____
_____
_____

Your ideal monthly financial budget.

The role of nature in your happiness.

How today would be different if you were rich and famous.

_____
_____
_____
_____
_____
_____
_____
_____
_____
_____
_____

How today would be different if you had a serious medical condition.

_____
_____
_____
_____
_____
_____
_____
_____
_____
_____
_____
_____
_____

Three reasons why you're absolutely good enough.

_____
_____
_____
_____
_____
_____
_____
_____
_____
_____
_____
_____
_____
_____

The trip you've always wanted to make.

_____
_____
_____
_____
_____
_____
_____
_____
_____
_____
_____
_____
_____
_____
_____
_____

"Love all, trust a few, do wrong to none."
William Shakespeare, *All's Well That Ends Well*

_____
_____
_____
_____
_____
_____
_____
_____
_____
_____
_____

How you could majorly improve your life
within the next three months.

_____
_____
_____
_____
_____
_____
_____
_____
_____
_____
_____
_____

The roadmap for learning a new skill.

_____
_____
_____
_____
_____
_____
_____
_____
_____
_____
_____
_____
_____
_____

The movies that more or less changed your life.

_____
_____
_____
_____
_____
_____
_____
_____
_____
_____
_____
_____
_____
_____
_____
_____

Fight or flight response?

_____
_____
_____
_____
_____
_____
_____
_____
_____
_____
_____
_____
_____

The influence of your parents in the making of your decisions.

_____
_____
_____
_____
_____
_____
_____
_____
_____
_____
_____
_____
_____
_____

What could you give away?

What guilty pleasure could develop into a bad habit?

Three character traits of a best friend.

_____
_____
_____
_____
_____
_____
_____
_____
_____
_____
_____
_____

Your life situation one year from now.

_____
_____
_____
_____
_____
_____
_____
_____
_____
_____
_____
_____
_____
_____
_____

"Time is the longest distance between two places."
Tennessee Williams, *The Glass Menagerie*

What in your life is actually an illusion?

A work schedule to be more productive in less time.

_____
_____
_____
_____
_____
_____
_____
_____
_____
_____
_____
_____
_____

If you let out your anger, what would it look like?

_____
_____
_____
_____
_____
_____
_____
_____
_____
_____
_____
_____
_____
_____

Describe your most attractive self.

_____
_____
_____
_____
_____
_____
_____
_____
_____
_____
_____
_____

The three character traits of a love partner.

_____
_____
_____
_____
_____
_____
_____
_____
_____
_____
_____
_____
_____
_____

What you perfect date night would look like.

_____
_____
_____
_____
_____
_____
_____
_____
_____
_____
_____
_____
_____

The three lessons you would share with your 12-year old self.

_____
_____
_____
_____
_____
_____
_____
_____
_____
_____
_____
_____
_____
_____
_____

Three titles for your autobiography.

_____
_____
_____
_____
_____
_____
_____
_____
_____
_____
_____
_____
_____
_____

"I felt my lungs inflate with the onrush of scenery—air, mountains, trees, people. I thought, "This is what it is to be happy."
Sylvia Plath, _The Bell Jar_

_____
_____
_____
_____
_____
_____
_____
_____
_____
_____
_____
_____
_____
_____

One of your most vivid dreams.

_____
_____
_____
_____
_____
_____
_____
_____
_____
_____
_____
_____
_____

Your biggest fear, transformed into a joke or satire.

_____
_____
_____
_____
_____
_____
_____
_____
_____
_____
_____
_____
_____
_____
_____

Three ways to improve your financial situation within one year.

_____
_____
_____
_____
_____
_____
_____
_____
_____
_____
_____
_____
_____

The last time you felt incredibly happy.

_____
_____
_____
_____
_____
_____
_____
_____
_____
_____
_____
_____
_____
_____

Three ways you could treat yourself without feeling guilty.

The last time you felt lonely.

How you would feel after an uncomfortable conversation.

_____
_____
_____
_____
_____
_____
_____
_____
_____
_____
_____
_____
_____

A place where you feel totally at peace.

_____
_____
_____
_____
_____
_____
_____
_____
_____
_____
_____
_____
_____
_____
_____

"Happiness is holding someone in your arms and knowing you hold the whole world."
Orhan Pamuk, Snow

_____
_____
_____
_____
_____
_____
_____
_____
_____
_____
_____
_____
_____
_____

How technology made your life better.

_____
_____
_____
_____
_____
_____
_____
_____
_____
_____
_____
_____
_____

The difference between courage and cowardness.

You at a networking event.

An honest Facebook status update of your current situation.

_____
_____
_____
_____
_____
_____
_____
_____
_____
_____
_____
_____

A secret that is influencing your life in a negative way.

_____
_____
_____
_____
_____
_____
_____
_____
_____
_____
_____
_____
_____

A dialogue between you and your Inner child.

_____
_____
_____
_____
_____
_____
_____
_____
_____
_____
_____
_____
_____
_____

Three things you could do to improve your sex life in a healthy way.

_____
_____
_____
_____
_____
_____
_____
_____
_____
_____
_____
_____
_____
_____

What you'd want to see before you die.

_____
_____
_____
_____
_____
_____
_____
_____
_____
_____
_____
_____

A situation where you were treated unfairly.

_____
_____
_____
_____
_____
_____
_____
_____
_____
_____
_____
_____
_____
_____

The definition of mindfulness.

_____

"Every heart sings a song,
incomplete, until another heart whispers back.
Those who wish to sing always find a song.
At the touch of a lover, everyone becomes a poet."
Plato

_____

The value of silence.

_____

_____

_____

_____

_____

_____

_____

_____

_____

_____

_____

_____

One of your stressful to-do-lists.

_____

_____

_____

_____

_____

_____

_____

_____

_____

_____

_____

_____

_____

_____

The value of christmas in your life.

_____
_____
_____
_____
_____
_____
_____
_____
_____
_____
_____
_____
_____

A weekly workout routine you could easily
follow for one month straight.

_____
_____
_____
_____
_____
_____
_____
_____
_____
_____
_____
_____
_____

what you would do when life would become too overwhelming.

_____

_____

_____

_____

_____

_____

_____

_____

_____

_____

_____

_____

_____

The difference between hearing and listening.

_____

_____

_____

_____

_____

_____

_____

_____

_____

_____

_____

_____

_____

Your favorite wardrobe.

_____
_____
_____
_____
_____
_____
_____
_____
_____
_____
_____
_____

A conversation between you and a high-school bully.

_____
_____
_____
_____
_____
_____
_____
_____
_____
_____
_____
_____
_____
_____

If you had made different choices five years ago...

_____
_____
_____
_____
_____
_____
_____
_____
_____
_____
_____

"What is that you express in your eyes? It seems to me more than all
the print I have read in my life."
Walt Whitman

_____
_____
_____
_____
_____
_____
_____
_____
_____
_____
_____
_____
_____

A dialogue between you and your ten-year older Self.

The influence of religion in your life.

A poem about your best friend.

_____

_____

_____

_____

_____

_____

_____

_____

_____

_____

_____

_____

Three things you want to do before you die.

_____

_____

_____

_____

_____

_____

_____

_____

_____

_____

_____

_____

_____

_____

You as a comic superhero.

_____

_____

_____

_____

_____

_____

_____

_____

_____

_____

_____

_____

_____

You and your family telling each other the truth.

_____

_____

_____

_____

_____

_____

_____

_____

_____

_____

_____

_____

_____

_____

_____

How you want to be remembered.

_____
_____
_____
_____
_____
_____
_____
_____
_____
_____
_____

"Of all forms of caution,
caution in love is perhaps the most fatal to true happiness."
Bertrand Russell, The Conquest of Happiness

_____
_____
_____
_____
_____
_____
_____
_____
_____
_____
_____
_____

what you would do with winning 100 thousand in the lottery.

_____
_____
_____
_____
_____
_____
_____
_____
_____
_____
_____
_____
_____

Three things you are grateful for.

_____
_____
_____
_____
_____
_____
_____
_____
_____
_____
_____
_____
_____
_____
_____
_____

What is hidden in your Shadow Self?

_____
_____
_____
_____
_____
_____
_____
_____
_____
_____
_____
_____
_____

All the social conditions that actually don't work for you.

_____
_____
_____
_____
_____
_____
_____
_____
_____
_____
_____
_____
_____
_____
_____

New rules of society if it were up to you.

_____
_____
_____
_____
_____
_____
_____
_____
_____
_____
_____
_____
_____
_____
_____

The three most frequent lies you tell about yourself.

_____
_____
_____
_____
_____
_____
_____
_____
_____
_____
_____
_____
_____
_____
_____
_____

How you could use your creativity to find more joy in your life.

_____
_____
_____
_____
_____
_____
_____
_____
_____
_____
_____
_____
_____
_____
_____

Three things you've always wanted to change in your house.

_____
_____
_____
_____
_____
_____
_____
_____
_____
_____
_____
_____
_____
_____
_____
_____
_____

If you would stop waiting.

"And now here is my secret, a very simple secret:
It is only with the heart that one can see rightly;
what is essential is invisible to the eye."
Antoine de Saint-Exupéry, The Little Prince

Your hidden talent in action.

_____
_____
_____
_____
_____
_____
_____
_____
_____
_____
_____
_____
_____

what your friends would say about you
in a documentary about your life.

_____
_____
_____
_____
_____
_____
_____
_____
_____
_____
_____
_____
_____

A diary page written by the 16-year old you.

_____
_____
_____
_____
_____
_____
_____
_____
_____
_____
_____
_____
_____

Five healthy things you love to eat.

_____
_____
_____
_____
_____
_____
_____
_____
_____
_____
_____
_____
_____
_____

You on a blind date.

_____
_____
_____
_____
_____
_____
_____
_____
_____
_____
_____
_____
_____

A dialogue between you and your Higher Self.

_____
_____
_____
_____
_____
_____
_____
_____
_____
_____
_____
_____
_____
_____
_____

If one of your bad habits was actually treated as an addiction.

_____
_____
_____
_____
_____
_____
_____
_____
_____
_____
_____
_____
_____
_____
_____

Your ideal budget for the next week.

Three things you would regret if you'd die right now.

_____
_____
_____
_____
_____
_____
_____
_____
_____
_____
_____
_____
_____

What you'd see if you stand naked in front of the mirror.

_____
_____
_____
_____
_____
_____
_____
_____
_____
_____
_____
_____
_____
_____

Three things you wish you knew five years ago.

_____
_____
_____
_____
_____
_____
_____
_____
_____
_____
_____
_____
_____
_____
_____
_____

What you'd see if you stand naked in front of the mirror.

_____
_____
_____
_____
_____
_____
_____
_____
_____
_____
_____
_____
_____
_____
_____
_____
_____

"Understanding is the first step to acceptance, and only with acceptance can there be recovery."
J.K. Rowling, Harry Potter and the Goblet of Fire

_____
_____
_____
_____
_____
_____
_____
_____
_____
_____
_____
_____
_____

The next step in your career.

_____
_____
_____
_____
_____
_____
_____
_____
_____
_____
_____
_____

If that were you constantly worried about, had a happy end.

_____
_____
_____
_____
_____
_____
_____
_____
_____
_____
_____
_____
_____
_____

Three things other people could learn from you
when it comes to friendships.

_____
_____
_____
_____
_____
_____
_____
_____
_____
_____
_____
_____
_____
_____

Three conversation starters, for meeting new people.

A dialogue between you and your boss.

Transform three of your biggest insecurities into persons.

_____
_____
_____
_____
_____
_____
_____
_____
_____
_____
_____
_____
_____
_____

What other people would definitely find attractive about you.

_____
_____
_____
_____
_____
_____
_____
_____
_____
_____
_____
_____
_____
_____
_____
_____

"Even if you are on the right track,
you'll get run over if you just sit there."
Will Rogers

_____
_____
_____
_____
_____
_____
_____
_____
_____
_____
_____
_____
_____
_____

complain about everything that's wrong with your life.

_____
_____
_____
_____
_____
_____
_____
_____
_____
_____
_____

If you would stand in the shoes of the people you dislike.

_____
_____
_____
_____
_____
_____
_____
_____
_____
_____
_____
_____
_____
_____

Three small things you could do to make your life easier.

_____
_____
_____
_____
_____
_____
_____
_____
_____
_____
_____
_____
_____
_____
_____

what you 80-year old Self would tell you now.

_____

_____

_____

_____

_____

_____

_____

_____

_____

_____

_____

If social anxiety wasn't a factor anymore...

_____

_____

_____

_____

_____

_____

_____

_____

_____

_____

_____

_____

Three things you could do to improve the relationship with yourself.

_____
_____
_____
_____
_____
_____
_____
_____
_____
_____
_____
_____
_____
_____

A poem about what strangers contributed to your life.

_____
_____
_____
_____
_____
_____
_____
_____
_____
_____
_____
_____
_____
_____
_____

"It was only a sunny smile, and little it cost in the giving, but like morning light it scattered the night and made the day worth living."
F. Scott Fitzgerald

_____
_____
_____
_____
_____
_____
_____
_____
_____
_____
_____
_____

If you would be totally honest for seven days straight.

_____
_____
_____
_____
_____
_____
_____
_____
_____
_____
_____
_____

The last time you were without worries and felt free and alive.

_____

Three things you want to say before you die.

_____

A dialogue between you and the universe.

Three titles for a self-help book you would write.

Your favorite strategy for dealing with insecurities.

_____
_____
_____
_____
_____
_____
_____
_____
_____
_____
_____
_____
_____
_____

A roadmap for success.

Three things you could do to make the world a better place.

The value of acceptance.

The last time you were humiliated.

_____
_____
_____
_____
_____
_____
_____
_____
_____
_____
_____
_____
_____
_____

A perfect day of relaxation.

_____
_____
_____
_____
_____
_____
_____
_____
_____
_____
_____
_____
_____
_____

"When people don't express themselves, they die one piece at a time."
Laurie Halse Anderson, *Speak*

If your biggest failure turned out to be a blessing.

what would happen if you showed your vulnerability?

_____
_____
_____
_____
_____
_____
_____
_____
_____
_____
_____
_____
_____

The last time you cried.

_____
_____
_____
_____
_____
_____
_____
_____
_____
_____
_____
_____
_____
_____

A master plan for dealing with the worst possible scenario if you'd (have to) quit your job within 6 months.

_____
_____
_____
_____
_____
_____
_____
_____
_____
_____
_____

Your definition of God.

_____
_____
_____
_____
_____
_____
_____
_____
_____
_____
_____
_____
_____

Five minutes inside the mind of someone you admire.

The difference between your thoughts, and who you really are.

"One love, one heart, one destiny."
Bob Marley

What is left unsaid...

The definition of *future*.

If you'd spoke from your heart to your (future) partner.

How your love life influences your everyday thoughts.

_____
_____
_____
_____
_____
_____
_____
_____
_____
_____
_____
_____
_____
_____
_____
_____

Three business ideas that could make you extra money.

_____
_____
_____
_____
_____
_____
_____
_____
_____
_____
_____
_____
_____
_____
_____
_____

One love scene that would make you cry.

_____
_____
_____
_____
_____
_____
_____
_____
_____
_____
_____
_____
_____
_____
_____
_____

One happy ending that would give you infinite hope.

_____
_____
_____
_____
_____
_____
_____
_____
_____
_____
_____
_____
_____
_____
_____
_____
_____

Your worst nightmare when it comes to your career.

_____

_____

_____

_____

_____

_____

_____

_____

_____

_____

_____

_____

_____

_____

Seven things that you'd love to do on a day off.

_____

_____

_____

_____

_____

_____

_____

_____

_____

_____

_____

_____

_____

_____

_____

_____

A quote you want to be remembered by.

_____
_____
_____
_____
_____
_____
_____
_____
_____
_____
_____
_____
_____

A plan for organizing a dinner party for friends and/or family.

_____
_____
_____
_____
_____
_____
_____
_____
_____
_____
_____
_____
_____
_____
_____
_____

The last time you really challenged yourself.

_____
_____
_____
_____
_____
_____
_____
_____
_____
_____
_____
_____
_____

Three lessons (your) kids should always remember.

_____
_____
_____
_____
_____
_____
_____
_____
_____
_____
_____
_____
_____
_____
_____

"You see things; you say, 'Why?'
But I dream things that never were; and I say 'Why not?'"
George Bernard Shaw, Back to Methuselah

_____
_____
_____
_____
_____
_____
_____
_____
_____
_____
_____
_____

A dialogue between you and your ex.

_____
_____
_____
_____
_____
_____
_____
_____
_____
_____
_____
_____

If your current life situation was a comedy.

_____
_____
_____
_____
_____
_____
_____
_____
_____
_____
_____
_____
_____

Three 'How To Books' you could write.

_____
_____
_____
_____
_____
_____
_____
_____
_____
_____
_____
_____
_____
_____

A short biography about yourself.

_____

_____

_____

_____

_____

_____

_____

_____

_____

_____

_____

_____

_____

_____

A short biography about how you'd want to be in the next three years.

_____

_____

_____

_____

_____

_____

_____

_____

_____

_____

_____

_____

_____

_____

_____

The first three things that would happen if you ruled the country.

The reason for your existence.

If you were the average of your five closest friends, you'd be...

_____
_____
_____
_____
_____
_____
_____
_____
_____
_____
_____
_____
_____
_____

Three reasons that make you an awesome lover.

_____
_____
_____
_____
_____
_____
_____
_____
_____
_____
_____
_____
_____
_____
_____

If you had seven million US dollars in your saving account...

_____
_____
_____
_____
_____
_____
_____
_____
_____
_____
_____
_____
_____

What kind of animal would you be and why?

_____
_____
_____
_____
_____
_____
_____
_____
_____
_____
_____
_____
_____
_____

If you were jobless and had enough money to pay the rent
and further necessities for six months.

_____
_____
_____
_____
_____
_____
_____
_____
_____
_____
_____
_____
_____

If you'd be back in High School, then...

_____
_____
_____
_____
_____
_____
_____
_____
_____
_____
_____
_____
_____

A healthy menu for the next seven days.

Describe your comfort zone.

"I am a part of all that I have met."
Alfred Tennyson

_____
_____
_____
_____
_____
_____
_____
_____
_____
_____
_____
_____
_____
_____
_____

The difference between your soul and your thoughts.

_____
_____
_____
_____
_____
_____
_____
_____
_____
_____
_____
_____
_____
_____

If you had control over your emotions, you would...

This actually makes you grateful, every day.

If you knew there is no way you could fail.

A dialogue between you and someone you dislike.

The reason you choose this career path.

_____
_____
_____
_____
_____
_____
_____
_____
_____
_____
_____
_____
_____
_____

The reason you have your current love life.

_____
_____
_____
_____
_____
_____
_____
_____
_____
_____
_____
_____
_____
_____

what your physical appearance says about you as a person.

_____

_____

_____

_____

_____

_____

_____

_____

_____

_____

_____

_____

_____

_____

_____

A dialogue between you and a bullied kid.

_____

_____

_____

_____

_____

_____

_____

_____

_____

_____

_____

_____

_____

_____

_____

what character would you play in a movie?

what part does 'change' play in your life?

Three things you could do to better adapt yourself to change.

_____
_____
_____
_____
_____
_____
_____
_____
_____
_____
_____
_____
_____
_____

A compliment you would give yourself.

_____
_____
_____
_____
_____
_____
_____
_____
_____
_____
_____
_____
_____
_____
_____
_____

A poem about joy.

What has adversity taught you so far?

Your favorite strategy for dealing with criticism.

_____
_____
_____
_____
_____
_____
_____
_____
_____
_____
_____
_____
_____

Through sadness and tears, there shines a small and ever glowing light.
The dark days have been and will be,
but never are they dark enough to dim the light.
It's in you. It's above you. It's around you.
c.w. v. Straaten

_____
_____
_____
_____
_____
_____
_____
_____
_____
_____
_____
_____

what life is trying to teach you all along?

_____
_____
_____
_____
_____
_____
_____
_____
_____
_____
_____
_____
_____
_____

If you would step away from your cloud of worries.

_____
_____
_____
_____
_____
_____
_____
_____
_____
_____
_____
_____
_____
_____
_____

Three things to do this week to make life more enjoyable.

_____
_____
_____
_____
_____
_____
_____
_____
_____
_____
_____
_____
_____
_____

The one advice you need right now.

_____
_____
_____
_____
_____
_____
_____
_____
_____
_____
_____
_____
_____

A letter to yourself, to be opened one year from now.

Personal Journal

About The Authors

We specialize in creating empowering, elegant & inspirational self-help journals. The power of journaling, of consistent self-reflection, is a scientifically proven habit that will benefit your life in truly astonishing ways. Mainly 90-Day or Yearly Journals, on various topics and for all types of people. Tools for self-reflection, gratitude & personal growth. We create each journal or workbook with the utmost care and the honest intention to give lasting benefit to our customers.

We hope to guide you through releasing limitations and discover your hidden potentials in all areas of life. And of course to give an enjoyable journaling experience. Step by step, to unlock the true you. Step by step, to a better world. We'd love to hear your ideas, tips, and questions. Let us know at exercises21@yahoo.com

Other Journals By 21 Exercises

The 365 Self-Discovery Journal:
One Year Of Reflection, Development & Happiness

The Daily Quote: Inspirations For A Calmer Mind

Courage, Love & Happiness: A Self-Discovery Journal For Women

The Self Exploration Journal: 90 Days of Writing, Discovery & Reflection

The Gratitude Journal: A Fresh New Start In 90 Days

The 365 Addiction Recovery Journal:
Daily Journaling With Guided Questions, To Become A New You

The Mindfulness Journal: A Calm Mind In 90 Days

If you want to buy one of these journals, you can go to the following page:
www.amazon.com/21-Exercises/e/B07RGJ1WVT

We are ready to serve you!

we wish you all the best!

The Writing Prompt Journal

A creative Self-Discovery Guide

Follow us on Instagram
For promotions, giveaways and newest arrivals

Instagram: 21exercises_journals

Made in the USA
Middletown, DE
16 September 2022